WEALTH WHISPERS

Insights into Successful Investing and Financial Growth

NANCY BARLOW

TABLE OF CONTENT

INTRODUCTION

In the vast landscape of finance and investment, navigating the terrain to achieve sustainable wealth can seem like a daunting task. Yet, hidden within the complexities lie whispers of wisdom that, when heeded, can illuminate the path to financial success. Welcome to "Wealth Whispers: Insights into Successful Investing and Financial Growth".

This book is not a magical formula promising overnight riches or speculative shortcuts to wealth. Instead, it is a comprehensive guide crafted from the collective wisdom of generations of investors, financial experts, and entrepreneurs. It's a roadmap designed to empower you with the knowledge and strategies necessary to make informed decisions, mitigate risks, and capitalize on opportunities in the dynamic world of finance.

"Wealth Whispers" is built upon the foundational principle that wealth creation is not solely about making money; it's about managing it effectively, growing it steadily, and ultimately achieving financial freedom. Through the pages of this book, you will embark on a journey that transcends mere accumulation of wealth, delving into the mindset, principles, and strategies that underpin enduring prosperity.

Whether you're a seasoned investor seeking to refine your approach or someone just beginning to explore the world of finance, this book is intended to be your trusted companion. Each chapter is meticulously crafted to provide actionable insights, practical advice, and real-world examples that resonate across various investment landscapes.

From understanding the fundamentals of investing to deciphering complex financial instruments, from building a diversified portfolio to navigating market volatility, "Wealth Whispers" equips you with the tools and knowledge necessary to thrive in any economic environment. Moreover, it emphasizes the importance of cultivating a mindset of abundance, discipline, and resilience—an indispensable trait for anyone aiming to attain lasting financial success.

As you embark on this journey through the pages of "Wealth Whispers," remember that wealth is not merely a destination but a journey—a journey marked by continuous learning, adaptability, and unwavering commitment to your financial goals. May the whispers of wisdom contained within these pages serve as your guiding light, illuminating the path towards a future of financial abundance and prosperity?

CHAPTER 1:

FOUNDATIONS OF

WEALTH CREATION

Before embarking on any journey, it's essential to understand the terrain, prepare the necessary supplies, and chart a course towards your destination. Similarly, in the realm of finance and investing, laying down a solid foundation is paramount to achieving long-term success and prosperity. Welcome to the first chapter of "Wealth Whispers: Insights into Successful Investing and Financial Growth," where we delve into the fundamental principles that underpin wealth creation.

In this chapter, we will embark on a journey of discovery, exploring the bedrock upon which financial success is built. From understanding the basics of investing to establishing clear financial goals, each section is crafted to provide you with the knowledge and tools necessary to lay a strong foundation for your financial future.

As we navigate through the complexities of wealth creation, remember that every great edifice begins with a single stone, every towering tree with a tiny seed. Similarly, your journey towards financial abundance starts with mastering the fundamentals, cultivating a mindset of abundance, and committing to your long-term financial goals.

So, let us embark on this enlightening journey together, as we uncover the timeless principles and strategies that form the bedrock of wealth creation. May the insights gained in this chapter serve as the cornerstone upon which you build a future of financial prosperity and abundance?

- Understanding the Basics of Investing

Investing is the act of committing money or capital to an endeavor with the expectation of generating income or profit. It is a fundamental aspect of wealth creation, allowing individuals to grow their assets over time. Understanding the basics of investing is crucial for anyone looking to build long-term financial security and achieve their financial goals. Here, we'll comprehensively discuss the essential concepts and principles of investing:

1. **Setting Investment Goals:** Before diving into the world of investing, it's vital to establish clear and realistic investment goals. These goals may include saving for retirement, purchasing a home, funding education, or achieving financial independence. Setting specific, measurable, achievable, relevant, and time-bound (SMART) goals helps provide direction and motivation for your investment journey.

2. **Risk and Return:** Investing inherently involves risk. Risk refers to the uncertainty of investment returns, including the potential for loss. Generally, investments with higher potential returns also carry higher levels of risk. Understanding your risk tolerance—the degree of comfort you have with fluctuations in the value of your investments—is

essential for constructing a suitable investment portfolio. Balancing risk and return is a key consideration in investment decision-making.

3. **Asset Classes:** Investments can be categorized into different asset classes, each with its unique characteristics and risk-return profiles. The primary asset classes include:

- **Equities (Stocks):** Ownership shares in publicly traded companies, offering potential for capital appreciation and dividends.

- **Fixed-Income Securities:** Debt instruments such as bonds and treasury bills, providing regular interest payments and principal repayment at maturity.

- **Real Estate:** Physical properties or real estate investment trusts (REITs), offering potential rental income and property appreciation.

- **Commodities:** Raw materials such as gold, silver, oil, and agricultural products, serving as hedges against inflation and geopolitical risks.

4. **Diversification:** Diversification is a risk management strategy that involves spreading investments across different asset classes, industries, geographic regions, and investment vehicles. By diversifying your portfolio, you can reduce the impact of adverse events on your overall investment returns. Asset allocation—the distribution of investments among various asset classes—plays a crucial role in diversification.

5. **Investment Vehicles:** There are various investment vehicles or instruments through which individuals can invest their money. These include:

- Individual Stocks

- Mutual Funds

- Exchange-traded funds (ETFs)

- Bonds

- Real Estate Investment Trusts (REITs)

- Retirement Accounts (e.g., 401(k), IRA)

- Savings Accounts

- Certificates of Deposit (CDs)

- Commodities and Precious Metals

6. **Time Horizon:** Your investment time horizon refers to the length of time you expect to hold an investment before needing to access the funds. Generally, longer time horizons allow for more aggressive investment strategies and greater tolerance for market volatility. Understanding your time horizon helps determine the appropriate investment vehicles and asset allocation for your goals.

7. **Costs and Fees:** When investing, it's essential to consider the costs and fees associated with different investment products and services. These may include brokerage commissions, mutual fund expense ratios, advisory fees, and transaction costs. Minimizing investment costs can significantly impact your overall investment returns over time.

8. **Monitoring and Rebalancing:** Investing is not a one-time activity but requires ongoing monitoring and periodic rebalancing of your investment

portfolio. Monitoring involves tracking the performance of your investments, staying informed about market developments, and evaluating whether your portfolio remains aligned with your investment goals and risk tolerance. Rebalancing involves adjusting your portfolio's asset allocation periodically to maintain desired risk levels and investment objectives.

In conclusion, mastering the basics of investing is essential for building a solid foundation for your financial future. By setting clear goals, understanding risk and return, diversifying your portfolio, choosing appropriate investment vehicles, and monitoring your investments regularly, you can navigate the complexities of the financial markets and work towards achieving your long-term financial objectives. Remember, investing is a journey that requires patience, discipline, and ongoing education to succeed.

- Importance of Financial Literacy

Financial literacy refers to the knowledge and skills necessary to make informed and effective decisions regarding money management, budgeting, saving, investing, and debt management. It empowers individuals to navigate the complexities of the financial world, make sound financial choices, and achieve their short-term and long-term financial goals. Here, we'll comprehensively discuss the significance of financial literacy:

1. **Personal Financial Management:** Financial literacy equips individuals with the knowledge and tools to effectively manage their finances. This includes creating and sticking to a budget, tracking income and expenses, understanding the importance of saving and managing debt responsibly. By practicing good financial habits, individuals can achieve greater financial stability and resilience in the face of economic challenges.

2. **Goal Setting and Planning:** Financial literacy enables individuals to set clear financial goals and develop actionable plans to achieve them. Whether it's saving for retirement, buying a home, funding education, or starting a business, understanding financial concepts allows individuals to create realistic goals, prioritize their financial objectives, and take steps towards realizing their aspirations.

3. **Investment Decision-Making:** Investing is a critical aspect of wealth building, but it can be intimidating for those lacking financial literacy. A strong foundation in financial concepts helps individuals understand different investment options, assess risk and return profiles, diversify their investment portfolios, and make informed investment decisions aligned with their financial goals and risk tolerance.

4. **Debt Management:** Debt can be a double-edged sword, providing access to capital but also carrying financial risks if not managed properly. Financial literacy enables individuals to understand the types of debt, evaluate the costs and benefits of

borrowing, develop strategies for debt repayment, and avoid high-interest debt traps. By managing debt wisely, individuals can minimize financial stress and work towards achieving financial freedom.

5. **Consumer Protection:** Financial literacy empowers individuals to make informed decisions as consumers. Understanding financial products and services, reading and interpreting financial statements, and recognizing deceptive practices help individuals safeguard their financial interests and avoid falling victim to scams or predatory financial schemes.

6. **Economic Participation and Empowerment:** Financial literacy is essential for fostering economic participation and empowerment. It enables individuals to access financial services, engage in economic activities, and contribute to economic growth and development. Moreover, financial literacy promotes financial inclusion by ensuring that all individuals, regardless of their

socioeconomic background, have the knowledge and skills to participate fully in the financial system.

7. **Long-Term Financial Security:** Ultimately, financial literacy plays a crucial role in building long-term financial security and resilience. By empowering individuals to make informed financial decisions, plan for the future, and adapt to changing economic circumstances, financial literacy helps mitigate financial risks, build wealth over time, and achieve financial independence.

In conclusion, financial literacy is a foundational skill that is essential for personal financial management, investment decision-making, debt management, consumer protection, economic empowerment, and long-term financial security. By promoting financial education and empowering individuals with the knowledge and skills to navigate the complexities of the financial world, we can build a more financially literate society and foster greater economic well-being for all.

- Building a Strong Financial Foundation

Building a strong financial foundation is crucial for achieving long-term financial stability, security, and prosperity. It involves establishing healthy financial habits, setting clear goals, and making informed decisions about money management, saving, investing, and debt management. Here, we'll comprehensively discuss the process of building a strong financial foundation:

1. **Assessing Financial Health:** The first step in building a strong financial foundation is to assess your current financial situation. This includes reviewing your income, expenses, assets, liabilities, and cash flow. By understanding your financial health, you can identify areas for improvement and develop strategies to achieve your financial goals.

2. **Setting Financial Goals:** Once you have assessed your financial situation, the next step is to set clear and achievable financial goals. These goals

may include saving for emergencies, paying off debt, buying a home, funding education, saving for retirement, or achieving financial independence. Setting specific, measurable, achievable, relevant, and time-bound (SMART) goals provides direction and motivation for your financial journey.

3. **Creating a Budget:** A budget is a critical tool for managing your finances and achieving your financial goals. It involves tracking your income and expenses, identifying areas where you can reduce spending or increase savings, and allocating funds towards your financial priorities. Creating and sticking to a budget helps you live within your means, avoid overspending, and build savings for the future.

4. **Emergency Fund:** Building an emergency fund is essential for financial security and resilience. An emergency fund is a savings account specifically set aside to cover unexpected expenses or financial emergencies, such as medical bills, car repairs, or job loss. Aim to save enough to cover three to six

months' worth of living expenses to provide a financial cushion in times of need.

5. **Managing Debt Wisely:** Debt can be a significant obstacle to building a strong financial foundation if not managed properly. Prioritize paying off high-interest debt, such as credit card debt or payday loans, as quickly as possible to reduce interest costs and free up funds for saving and investing. Consider consolidating or refinancing debt to lower interest rates and accelerate debt repayment.

6. **Saving and Investing:** Saving and investing are key components of building wealth over time. Establish a systematic approach to saving by automating contributions to your savings and investment accounts. Consider opening retirement accounts, such as a 401(k) or IRA, to take advantage of tax benefits and employer-matching contributions. Diversify your investment portfolio across different asset classes to manage risk and maximize returns over the long term.

7. **Insurance Protection:** Insurance plays a vital role in protecting your financial assets and mitigating risks. Ensure you have adequate insurance coverage, including health insurance, life insurance, disability insurance, and property and casualty insurance, to safeguard against unforeseen events that could derail your financial goals.

8. **Continual Learning and Adjustment:** Building a strong financial foundation is an ongoing process that requires continual learning and adjustment. Stay informed about financial best practices, investment strategies, and economic trends. Regularly review and adjust your financial plan as your goals, priorities, and circumstances change over time.

In conclusion, building a strong financial foundation is a multifaceted process that involves assessing your financial health, setting clear goals, creating a budget, building an emergency fund, managing debt wisely, saving and investing, obtaining insurance protection, and continually learning and adjusting. By implementing sound financial habits and making informed decisions, you can lay the groundwork for long-term financial security, stability, and prosperity.

- Setting Clear Financial Goals

Setting clear financial goals is a crucial step in achieving financial success and realizing your long-term aspirations. Clear financial goals provide direction, motivation, and focus for your financial planning efforts, guiding your decisions on saving, spending, investing, and debt management. Here, we'll comprehensively discuss the process of setting clear financial goals:

1. **Reflect on Your Values and Priorities:** Before setting financial goals, take the time to reflect on your values, priorities, and aspirations. Consider what matters most to you in life, both personally and professionally. Are you prioritizing homeownership, education, travel, entrepreneurship, or early retirement?

Understanding your values and priorities will help you align your financial goals with your broader life goals.

2. **Identify Short-Term and Long-Term Goals:** Financial goals can be categorized into short-term, medium-term, and long-term objectives. Short-term goals typically have a timeframe of one year or less and may include building an emergency fund, paying off high-interest debt, or saving for a vacation. Medium-term goals have a timeframe of one to five years and may include saving for a down payment on a home or funding a child's education. Long-term goals have a timeframe of five years or more and may include saving for retirement or achieving financial independence.

3. **Make Your Goals Specific, Measurable, Achievable, Relevant, and Time-Bound (SMART):** Use the SMART criteria to make your financial goals clear, actionable, and achievable:

- **Specific:** Clearly define what you want to accomplish, why it's important, and how you plan to achieve it.

- **Measurable:** Set concrete criteria for measuring progress towards your goals, such as specific dollar amounts or timelines.

- **Achievable:** Ensure that your goals are realistic and attainable given your financial resources, time constraints, and other commitments.

- **Relevant:** Align your goals with your values, priorities, and life aspirations to ensure they are meaningful and relevant to your overall well-being.

- **Time-Bound:** Establish deadlines or target dates for achieving your goals to create a sense of urgency and accountability.

4. **Quantify Your Goals:** Assign specific dollar amounts or numerical targets to your financial goals to make them tangible and measurable. For example, instead of simply aiming to "save for retirement," specify a target retirement savings amount or a desired retirement age. Quantifying

your goals allows you to track progress and adjust your financial plan as needed.

5. **Prioritize Your Goals:** Not all financial goals are equally urgent or important. Prioritize your goals based on their significance, time sensitivity, and feasibility. Focus on tackling high-priority goals first before addressing lower-priority objectives. Consider the potential trade-offs and opportunity costs of pursuing different goals simultaneously.

6. **Break Down Larger Goals into Smaller Milestones:** Large or long-term goals can seem daunting or overwhelming. Break down larger goals into smaller, manageable milestones or action steps. This allows you to make steady progress towards your goals and celebrate achievements along the way, keeping you motivated and focused on the ultimate objective.

7. **Review and Update Your Goals Regularly:** Financial goals are not set in stone and may evolve as your circumstances, priorities, and aspirations

change. Review and update your goals regularly to reflect changes in your life, financial situation, or external factors such as economic conditions or regulatory changes. Revisit your goals annually or as needed to ensure they remain relevant, achievable, and aligned with your values and priorities.

In conclusion, setting clear financial goals is a critical step in achieving financial success and realizing your dreams. By reflecting on your values and priorities, identifying specific and measurable goals, making them SMART, quantifying and prioritizing your goals, breaking them down into manageable milestones, and regularly reviewing and updating them, you can create a roadmap for financial prosperity and fulfillment.

CHAPTER 2: THE MINDSET OF SUCCESSFUL INVESTORS

Welcome to the chapter dedicated to exploring the mindset of successful investors. In the world of finance, achieving success goes beyond merely mastering technical analysis or picking the right stocks. It requires cultivating a mindset characterized by discipline, resilience, patience, and a willingness to embrace risk.

In this chapter, we delve into the psychological and emotional aspects of investing, recognizing that while numbers and charts are crucial, it's often our mindset that determines our success in the market. We'll explore the attitudes, beliefs, and behaviors that distinguish successful investors from the rest, offering insights and strategies to help you develop a mindset conducive to achieving your financial goals.

From overcoming common psychological biases to embracing uncertainty and volatility as opportunities rather than obstacles, the journey towards becoming a successful investor is as much about mastering your mind as it is about mastering the markets. We'll uncover the myths and misconceptions that often cloud investors' judgment and explore practical techniques for cultivating a mindset of abundance, patience, and long-term thinking.

Whether you're a seasoned investor looking to refine your approach or someone just starting to dip their toes into the world of finance, understanding the mindset of successful investors is essential for navigating the complexities of the market with confidence and conviction. So, join us as we embark on a journey of self-discovery and exploration, unlocking the secrets to mastering the mindset of successful investors and realizing your full potential in the world of finance.

- Cultivating an Abundance Mindset

Cultivating an abundance mindset is essential for achieving success in various aspects of life, including finances. An abundance mindset is characterized by optimism, gratitude, resilience, and a belief in limitless opportunities. It involves shifting your focus from scarcity and limitations to abundance and possibilities. Here, we'll comprehensively discuss the process of cultivating an abundance mindset:

1. **Awareness and Mindfulness:** The first step in cultivating an abundance mindset is to become aware of your thoughts, beliefs, and attitudes towards money and abundance. Practice mindfulness techniques such as meditation, journaling, or self-reflection to observe your thought patterns and identify any scarcity-based beliefs or fears that may be holding you back.

2. **Challenge Scarcity Mentality:** Scarcity mentality is characterized by a fear of lack and a belief that there are limited resources or opportunities available. Challenge scarcity-based thoughts and beliefs by reframing them into abundance-based perspectives. Instead of focusing on what you lack, shift your focus to what you have and what is possible. Practice gratitude for the abundance already present in your life, whether it's relationships, health, opportunities, or resources.

3. **Visualize Success and Abundance:** Visualization is a powerful technique for manifesting abundance and success. Spend time visualizing your goals and aspirations as if they have already been achieved. Imagine yourself living a life of abundance, experiencing financial freedom, and achieving your wildest dreams. Visualizing success helps reinforce positive beliefs and attitudes towards abundance, making it easier to manifest in your life.

4. **Surround Yourself with Positivity:** Surround yourself with positive influences and like-minded

individuals who embody an abundance mindset. Avoid negative people or environments that perpetuate scarcity thinking and limit your potential. Seek out mentors, coaches, or supportive communities that inspire and uplift you on your journey towards abundance.

5. **Embrace Failure and Learn from Setbacks:** Failure is an inevitable part of any journey towards success. Instead of viewing failure as a sign of scarcity or defeat, embrace it as an opportunity for growth and learning. Adopt a growth mindset, believing that setbacks are temporary and that you have the power to overcome obstacles and achieve your goals. Extract lessons from failures and use them as stepping stones towards greater success and abundance.

6. **Take Action and Seize Opportunities:** Cultivating an abundance mindset is not just about positive thinking; it also requires taking proactive steps towards your goals. Seize opportunities as they arise, even if they come with risks or uncertainties. Trust in your abilities and the

abundance of opportunities available to you. Be open-minded and flexible, willing to explore new avenues and embrace change as a catalyst for growth and abundance.

7. **Practice Generosity and Giving:** Generosity is a hallmark of an abundance mindset. Practice giving back to others through acts of kindness, charity, or volunteering. When you give freely without expecting anything in return, you reinforce the belief that there is more than enough to go around and that abundance is a renewable resource. By contributing to the well-being of others, you create a ripple effect of abundance that enriches both your life and the lives of those around you.

8. **Celebrate Successes and Milestones:** Finally, celebrate your successes and milestones along the way. Acknowledge and appreciate your progress, no matter how small. Celebrating successes reinforces positive behaviors and attitudes, reinforcing your belief in your ability to create abundance in your life.

In conclusion, cultivating an abundance mindset is a transformative journey that requires awareness, intentionality, and practice. By challenging scarcity-based beliefs, visualizing success, surrounding yourself with positivity, embracing failure, taking action, practicing generosity, and celebrating successes, you can shift your mindset from scarcity to abundance and unlock your full potential for success and fulfillment in all areas of your life, including finances.

- Overcoming Common Psychological Biases

Overcoming common psychological biases is essential for making sound investment decisions and achieving financial success. Psychological biases are cognitive shortcuts or mental tendencies that can lead to irrational behavior, distorted perceptions, and poor decision-making. Recognizing and addressing these biases is crucial for investors to avoid costly mistakes and navigate the financial markets effectively. Here, we'll comprehensively discuss the process of overcoming common psychological biases:

1. **Awareness and Education:** The first step in overcoming psychological biases is to become aware of their existence and understand how they can influence your decision-making process. Educate yourself about common biases that affect investors, such as confirmation bias, overconfidence, loss aversion, herd mentality, and recency bias. By understanding the psychological principles behind these biases, you can better recognize them when they arise in your thinking.

2. **Practice Self-awareness and Reflection:** Develop self-awareness by reflecting on your thoughts, emotions, and behaviors related to investing. Pay attention to times when you feel strong emotions such as fear, greed, or euphoria, as these can indicate the presence of biases. Regularly examine your investment decisions and assess whether they are based on rational analysis or influenced by emotional biases.

3. Challenge Assumptions and Question Your Decisions: Actively challenge assumptions and question your decisions to mitigate the impact of biases. Instead of relying solely on gut feelings or intuition, seek evidence-based reasoning and objective data to support your investment decisions. Consider alternative viewpoints and perspectives to avoid falling victim to confirmation bias, which involves seeking out information that confirms your pre-existing beliefs while ignoring contradictory evidence.

4. Develop a Systematic Decision-making Process: Implement a systematic decision-making process to reduce the influence of biases. Establish clear criteria and guidelines for evaluating investment opportunities, such as fundamental analysis, technical analysis, or a combination of both. Use checklists or decision-making frameworks to ensure that you consider all relevant factors and avoid making impulsive or emotionally driven decisions.

5. **Diversify Your Portfolio:** Diversification is a powerful strategy for mitigating the impact of psychological biases on investment outcomes. By spreading your investments across different asset classes, industries, and geographic regions, you can reduce the risk of individual investment decisions being influenced by biases. Diversification helps protect your portfolio from the adverse effects of specific market events or economic conditions.

6. **Seek Objective Advice and Feedback:** Consult with trusted financial advisors, mentors, or peers to gain objective advice and feedback on your investment decisions. A second opinion can provide valuable insights and help counteract the influence of biases. Surround yourself with individuals who can challenge your assumptions and offer constructive criticism, helping you make more rational and informed decisions.

7. **Implement Risk Management Strategies:** Incorporate risk management strategies into your investment approach to protect against potential losses resulting from psychological biases. Set clear

risk tolerance levels and establish stop-loss orders or exit strategies to limit downside risk. Avoid making emotional decisions in response to short-term market fluctuations and maintain a long-term perspective on your investment objectives.

8. **Continuous Learning and Improvement:** Overcoming psychological biases is an ongoing process that requires continuous learning and improvement. Stay informed about behavioral finance research and insights to deepen your understanding of how psychological biases impact investment behavior. Commit to lifelong learning and personal development to sharpen your decision-making skills and enhance your ability to overcome biases effectively.

In conclusion, overcoming common psychological biases is essential for making rational investment decisions and achieving long-term financial success. By cultivating self-awareness, challenging assumptions, developing systematic decision-making processes, diversifying your portfolio, seeking objective advice, implementing risk management strategies, and continuously learning and improving, you can mitigate the impact of biases and enhance your ability to navigate the financial markets with confidence and resilience.

- Developing Patience and Discipline

Developing patience and discipline is essential for achieving success in any endeavor, including investing. In the realm of finance, where volatility and uncertainty are prevalent, patience and discipline play a crucial role in maintaining a long-term perspective, sticking to your investment strategy, and avoiding impulsive decisions that can derail your financial goals. Here, we'll comprehensively discuss the process of developing patience and discipline:

1. **Clarify Your Financial Goals:** The first step in developing patience and discipline is to clarify your financial goals. Understand what you're striving to achieve with your investments, whether it's saving

for retirement, purchasing a home, funding education, or achieving financial independence. Having clear, specific goals provides a sense of purpose and direction, motivating you to stay disciplined and patient in pursuit of your objectives.

2. **Educate Yourself About Investing:** Knowledge is a powerful tool for building confidence and discipline in investing. Educate yourself about investment principles, strategies, and market dynamics to develop a deeper understanding of how financial markets operate. The more you know, the better equipped you'll be to make informed decisions and resist the urge to react impulsively to market fluctuations or short-term noise.

3. **Establish an Investment Plan**: Develop a well-thought-out investment plan that aligns with your financial goals, risk tolerance, and time horizon. Establish clear guidelines for asset allocation, diversification, and rebalancing to maintain a disciplined approach to investing. Stick to your investment plan through market ups and downs, avoiding knee-jerk reactions based on fear or greed.

4. **Set Realistic Expectations:** Recognize that investing is a long-term endeavor that requires patience and perseverance. Understand that achieving meaningful returns takes time and that there will inevitably be periods of market volatility and uncertainty along the way. Set realistic expectations for your investment performance and avoid chasing unrealistic returns or trying to time the market.

5. **Practice Delayed Gratification:** Cultivate the habit of delayed gratification by resisting the temptation to make impulsive decisions based on short-term impulses or emotions. Instead of seeking instant gratification, focus on the long-term benefits of staying disciplined and patient with your investments. Remind yourself of your overarching financial goals and the importance of staying the course, even when faced with temporary setbacks or market fluctuations.

6. **Develop Emotional Resilience:** Emotional resilience is the ability to withstand adversity and maintain composure in the face of challenges or

setbacks. Cultivate emotional resilience by managing stress, practicing mindfulness techniques, and developing coping strategies for dealing with market volatility or unexpected events. Recognize that fluctuations in the market are a normal part of investing and that maintaining a disciplined approach is key to long-term success.

7. **Monitor Your Progress and Adjust as Needed:** Regularly monitor your investment portfolio's performance and progress towards your financial goals. Review your investment plan periodically and make adjustments as needed based on changes in your circumstances, goals, or market conditions. However, avoid making frequent changes or reacting impulsively to short-term fluctuations, as this can undermine your long-term investment strategy.

8. **Celebrate Milestones and Stay Motivated:** Celebrate milestones along the way to achieving your financial goals, whether it's reaching a savings target, achieving a certain investment return, or paying off debt. Recognize and acknowledge your

progress to stay motivated and reinforce your commitment to patience and discipline. Celebrating milestones helps maintain momentum and encourages you to stay focused on your long-term objectives.

In conclusion, developing patience and discipline is essential for achieving success in investing and reaching your financial goals. By clarifying your financial objectives, educating yourself about investing, establishing a disciplined investment plan, setting realistic expectations, practicing delayed gratification, cultivating emotional resilience, monitoring your progress, and celebrating milestones, you can build the patience and discipline necessary to navigate the ups and downs of the financial markets and achieve long-term financial success.

- Embracing Risk as an Opportunity

Embracing risk as an opportunity is a fundamental mindset shift that is crucial for achieving success in investing and pursuing financial growth. Rather than viewing risk as something to be feared or avoided, embracing risk involves recognizing it as an inherent aspect of investing and seeing it as a potential source of opportunity and reward. Here, we'll comprehensively discuss the process of embracing risk as an opportunity:

1. **Understanding Risk:** The first step in embracing risk as an opportunity is to understand what risk entails. Risk in investing refers to the uncertainty or variability of investment returns, including the possibility of losing money or failing to achieve expected returns. Different types of risk exist, including market risk, inflation risk, interest rate risk, credit risk, and geopolitical risk. Understanding the various types of risk and their

potential impact on investment outcomes is essential for making informed decisions.

2. **Assessing Risk Tolerance:** Assess your risk tolerance, which is the degree of comfort you have with taking on risk in your investment portfolio. Risk tolerance is influenced by factors such as your financial goals, time horizon, investment knowledge, and emotional temperament. Recognize that risk tolerance is subjective and may vary from person to person. Conduct a risk assessment to determine your risk tolerance level and ensure that your investment strategy aligns with your comfort level.

3. **Balancing Risk and Reward:** Embracing risk involves striking a balance between risk and reward. Understand that higher levels of risk are typically associated with the potential for higher returns, but also come with increased volatility and the possibility of greater losses. Assess your risk-return tradeoff preferences and determine the level of risk that you are willing to accept in pursuit of your financial goals. Consider your investment

objectives, time horizon, and liquidity needs when evaluating risk-reward tradeoffs.

4. **Diversification:** Diversification is a key risk management strategy that involves spreading your investments across different asset classes, industries, and geographic regions. By diversifying your portfolio, you can reduce the impact of individual investment risks and mitigate the potential for significant losses. Embrace diversification as a way to manage risk effectively while still capitalizing on opportunities for growth and returns in the market.

5. **Viewing Volatility as Normal:** Embrace volatility as a normal and inevitable part of investing. Recognize that markets are inherently unpredictable and subject to fluctuations in response to various economic, political, and social factors. Rather than fearing volatility, see it as an opportunity to capitalize on market inefficiencies, exploit mispricings, and accumulate assets at discounted prices. Maintain a long-term perspective and focus on the underlying fundamentals of your

investments rather than short-term fluctuations in prices.

6. **Staying Informed and Adaptable:** Embracing risk requires staying informed about market developments, economic trends, and industry dynamics. Keep abreast of relevant news and information that may impact your investments. Be adaptable and willing to adjust your investment strategy in response to changing market conditions or new opportunities. Embrace uncertainty as an inherent aspect of investing and remain open to revising your views and strategies based on new information.

7. **Taking Calculated Risks:** Embracing risk does not mean being reckless or impulsive. Instead, it involves taking calculated risks based on thorough analysis and research. Conduct due diligence before making investment decisions, assess the potential risks and rewards and weigh the probabilities of various outcomes. Maintain a disciplined approach to risk-taking and avoid succumbing to emotions or herd mentality.

8. Learning from Failure and Resilience:
Embrace failure as a learning opportunity and a natural part of the investment process. Recognize that not all investments will be successful, and setbacks are inevitable along the way. Develop resilience and perseverance in the face of adversity, using failures as opportunities to refine your investment approach and improve your decision-making skills. Embrace risk as a necessary aspect of growth and innovation, and view setbacks as stepping stones towards greater success.

In conclusion, embracing risk as an opportunity is a mindset shift that is essential for achieving success in investing and pursuing financial growth. By understanding risk, assessing your risk tolerance, balancing risk and reward, diversifying your portfolio, viewing volatility as normal, staying informed and adaptable, taking calculated risks, and learning from failure and resilience, you can harness the power of risk to capitalize on opportunities and achieve your long-term financial goals.

CHAPTER 3:
STRATEGIES FOR
BUILDING WEALTH

Welcome to the chapter dedicated to exploring strategies for building wealth. In a world where financial security and independence are highly valued, understanding effective wealth-building strategies is essential for achieving long-term financial success. This chapter is designed to provide you with practical insights, techniques, and approaches to accumulate wealth, create financial stability, and achieve your financial goals.

Building wealth is not solely about earning a high income or lucking into windfall gains; it's about making strategic decisions and adopting disciplined habits that lead to sustainable financial growth over time. In this chapter, we'll explore a range of proven strategies and principles for building wealth, from saving and investing to entrepreneurship and passive income generation.

Whether you're just starting your wealth-building journey or looking to enhance your existing financial plan, this chapter offers valuable guidance and inspiration to help you navigate the complexities of wealth accumulation. By implementing the strategies outlined here and staying committed to your financial goals, you can lay the foundation for a future of prosperity, security, and abundance.

So, join us as we embark on this enlightening exploration of strategies for building wealth. Whether you're seeking to grow your savings, invest in the stock market, start a business, or explore alternative income streams, this chapter has something for everyone aspiring to achieve financial freedom and unlock the secrets of wealth creation.

- Diversification: Spreading Your Risks

Diversification is a fundamental strategy in investing that involves spreading your investment across different asset classes, industries, geographic regions, and investment vehicles to reduce risk and optimize returns. By diversifying your portfolio, you can mitigate the impact of individual investment losses and enhance the overall stability and resilience of your investments. Here, we'll comprehensively discuss diversification and the importance of spreading your risks:

1. **Risk Reduction:** One of the primary objectives of diversification is to reduce risk in your investment portfolio. By spreading your investments across a diverse range of assets, you can minimize the impact of any single investment's poor performance or adverse events on your overall portfolio. Diversification helps smooth out volatility and provides a buffer against market downturns,

economic uncertainties, and other external factors that can affect investment returns.

2. **Asset Class Diversification:** Diversifying across different asset classes is a cornerstone of portfolio diversification. Common asset classes include stocks (equities), bonds (fixed-income securities), real estate, cash equivalents, and alternative investments such as commodities or private equity. Each asset class has its unique risk-return profile, correlation with market trends, and response to economic conditions. By allocating your investments across multiple asset classes, you can balance the potential for growth with the need for stability and income.

3. **Industry and Sector Diversification:** Within each asset class, diversify your investments across different industries and sectors to minimize sector-specific risks. Industries and sectors may perform differently under various economic conditions and market cycles. For example, while technology companies may thrive during periods of innovation and growth, consumer staples companies may

demonstrate stability and resilience during economic downturns. Diversifying across industries helps spread your risks and capitalize on opportunities in different sectors of the economy.

4. **Geographic Diversification:** Geographic diversification involves investing in assets located in different geographic regions or countries. Different regions may experience varying economic growth rates, political stability, currency fluctuations, and regulatory environments. By diversifying globally, you can reduce your exposure to country-specific risks and benefit from opportunities in international markets. Geographic diversification also helps protect your portfolio against localized events or geopolitical risks that may impact specific regions.

5. **Investment Vehicle Diversification:** Diversify your investments across different types of investment vehicles or instruments to achieve a balanced portfolio. Common investment vehicles include individual stocks, mutual funds, exchange-traded funds (ETFs), bonds, real estate investment

trusts (REITs), and alternative investments such as hedge funds or venture capital funds. Each investment vehicle offers unique features, risk-return profiles, and tax implications. By diversifying across investment vehicles, you can access a broader range of opportunities and tailor your portfolio to your specific investment objectives and preferences.

6. **Rebalancing and Monitoring:** Regularly monitor your investment portfolio and rebalance as needed to maintain diversification and align with your investment goals. Market fluctuations and changes in economic conditions may cause your portfolio's asset allocation to drift over time. Rebalancing involves adjusting your portfolio's asset allocation periodically to bring it back in line with your target allocation. Rebalancing ensures that you continue to spread your risks effectively and capitalize on opportunities for growth while minimizing the impact of market volatility.

7. **Long-Term Perspective:** Diversification is a long-term strategy that requires patience, discipline,

and a focus on the big picture. While diversification can help mitigate short-term volatility and minimize the impact of individual investment losses, it's essential to maintain a long-term perspective and stay committed to your investment plan. Avoid making impulsive decisions based on short-term market fluctuations or trying to time the market. Instead, focus on building a well-diversified portfolio that aligns with your investment goals and risk tolerance over the long term.

In conclusion, diversification is a critical strategy for spreading your risks and optimizing returns in investing. By diversifying across asset classes, industries, geographic regions, and investment vehicles, you can reduce the impact of individual investment losses, smooth out volatility, and enhance the overall stability and resilience of your investment portfolio. Embrace diversification as a cornerstone of your investment strategy and a key component of long-term financial success.

- Value Investing vs. Growth Investing

Value investing and growth investing are two distinct investment approaches that reflect different philosophies and strategies for selecting and managing investment portfolios. While both approaches aim to generate positive returns for investors, they have unique characteristics, considerations, and objectives. Here, we'll comprehensively discuss value investing vs. growth investing:

Value Investing:

1. **Investment Philosophy:** Value investing is based on the principle of purchasing stocks that are trading at a price below their intrinsic value. The core philosophy of value investing is to identify undervalued companies that have strong fundamentals but are temporarily out of favor with the market.

2. **Focus on Fundamental Analysis:** Value investors focus on conducting thorough fundamental analysis of companies, including evaluating financial statements, assessing business fundamentals, analyzing competitive advantages, and estimating intrinsic value. They seek to identify companies with solid earnings, stable cash flows, low debt levels, and attractive valuation metrics such as low price-to-earnings (P/E) ratios, low price-to-book (P/B) ratios, or high dividend yields.

3. **Margin of Safety:** A key principle of value investing is the concept of margin of safety, which involves purchasing assets at a significant discount to their intrinsic value to provide a buffer against downside risk. Value investors seek to protect their capital by investing in companies with a wide margin of safety, minimizing the risk of permanent loss of capital.

4. **Long-Term Perspective:** Value investing is typically associated with a long-term investment horizon. Value investors are patient and disciplined, willing to wait for the market to recognize the

underlying value of their investments over time. They believe that the market will eventually reflect the intrinsic value of undervalued companies, leading to capital appreciation.

5. **Contrarian Approach:** Value investors often adopt a contrarian approach, which involves going against the prevailing market sentiment and investing in companies that are currently out of favor or facing temporary challenges. By taking a contrarian stance, value investors aim to capitalize on mispricings in the market and exploit opportunities for undervalued securities.

Growth Investing:

1. **Investment Philosophy:** Growth investing focuses on identifying companies with strong growth potential and earnings momentum. The core philosophy of growth investing is to invest in companies that are expected to grow their earnings and revenues at an above-average rate compared to the broader market.

2. Emphasis on Future Growth Prospects:
Growth investors prioritize future growth prospects and invest in companies that demonstrate strong revenue growth, expanding profit margins, innovative products or services, and a competitive edge in their respective industries. They are less concerned with current valuation metrics and more focused on the company's long-term growth potential.

3. **High Valuation Tolerances:** Growth investors are often willing to pay higher valuations for companies with strong growth prospects, even if their current earnings multiples appear elevated. They believe that investing in high-growth companies with attractive growth prospects justifies paying a premium price, as long as the company can sustain its growth trajectory over the long term.

4. **Focus on Momentum and Trends:** Growth investors pay close attention to market trends, industry dynamics, and emerging technologies that drive growth opportunities. They seek to identify companies that are positioned to benefit from

secular trends and disruptive innovations, aiming to capture significant upside potential as these companies continue to grow and expand their market share.

5. **Flexibility and Adaptability:** Growth investors are often more flexible and adaptable in their investment approach, willing to adjust their portfolios in response to changing market conditions or shifts in industry dynamics. They may actively trade or rotate their holdings to capitalize on short-term opportunities or emerging growth trends.

Key Considerations and Differences:

- **Risk and Return Profiles:** Value investing tends to be associated with lower risk and lower volatility compared to growth investing, as value stocks often have more stable earnings and lower valuations. However, growth investing offers the potential for higher returns over the long term, as successful growth companies can deliver significant capital appreciation.

- Market Cycles and Economic Conditions:
Value investing tends to perform well during
periods of economic uncertainty or market
downturns, as investors flock to defensive sectors
and undervalued stocks. In contrast, growth
investing thrives in bull markets and economic
expansions, as investors seek out high-growth
opportunities and riskier assets.

- Investor Preferences and Objectives: The choice
between value investing and growth investing
depends on individual investor preferences, risk
tolerance, and investment objectives. Value
investors may prioritize capital preservation and
income generation, while growth investors may
prioritize capital appreciation and wealth
accumulation over the long term.

In conclusion, value investing and growth investing
represent two distinct approaches to investing, each
with its philosophy, strategies, and objectives.
While value investing focuses on identifying
undervalued companies with strong fundamentals,
growth investing prioritizes companies with high

growth potential and earnings momentum. Both approaches have their merits and drawbacks, and the choice between them depends on individual investor preferences, risk tolerance, and investment goals. Ultimately, a well-diversified portfolio may incorporate elements of both value and growth investing to optimize risk-adjusted returns and achieve long-term financial success.

- Asset Allocation: Finding the Right Mix

Asset allocation is a critical component of investment strategy that involves diversifying investments across different asset classes to achieve a balance between risk and return. It is the process of determining the optimal mix of asset classes, such as stocks, bonds, cash, and alternative investments, based on an investor's financial goals, risk tolerance, time horizon, and investment objectives. Here, we'll comprehensively discuss asset allocation and the importance of finding the right mix:

1. **Understanding Asset Classes:** Asset classes are broad categories of investments that have similar risk and return characteristics. Common asset classes include:

   - **Stocks (Equities):** Ownership stakes in publicly traded companies, offering the potential for capital appreciation and dividends but also carrying higher volatility and risk.

   - **Bonds (Fixed-Income Securities):** Debt instruments issued by governments, corporations, or municipalities, providing regular interest payments and the return of principal at maturity, with lower volatility and risk compared to stocks.

   - **Cash Equivalents:** Short-term, low-risk investments such as money market funds, certificates of deposit (CDs), or Treasury bills, offering liquidity and stability but lower returns.

   - **Alternative Investments:** Non-traditional assets such as real estate, commodities, hedge funds, private equity, or cryptocurrencies, offering diversification and potential returns that are less correlated with traditional asset classes.

2. **Risk and Return Relationship:** Asset allocation is guided by the risk-return tradeoff, which suggests that higher expected returns are generally associated with higher levels of risk. Stocks typically offer the highest potential returns but also carry the highest level of volatility and risk. Bonds and cash equivalents provide lower returns but offer greater stability and downside protection. Alternative investments may offer unique risk-return profiles and diversification benefits compared to traditional asset classes.

3. **Investor Profile and Objectives:** Asset allocation should be tailored to an investor's profile, including their financial goals, risk tolerance, time horizon, and liquidity needs. Younger investors with longer time horizons and higher risk tolerance may allocate a larger portion of their portfolio to stocks to capitalize on long-term growth potential. In contrast, older investors or those with shorter

time horizons may allocate more to bonds and cash equivalents to preserve capital and generate income.

4. **Diversification Benefits:** Asset allocation provides diversification benefits by spreading investment across different asset classes that have low or negative correlations with each other. Diversification helps reduce portfolio volatility and minimize the impact of individual investment losses on overall portfolio performance. By combining assets with different risk-return profiles, investors can achieve a more balanced and resilient portfolio that can weather various market conditions.

5. **Strategic vs. Tactical Asset Allocation:** Asset allocation can be implemented through strategic or tactical approaches:

- **Strategic Asset Allocation:** Involves establishing a long-term target asset allocation based on an investor's financial goals and risk tolerance. Strategic asset allocation aims to maintain a consistent mix of asset classes over time, periodically rebalancing the portfolio to realign with the target allocation.

- **Tactical Asset Allocation:** Involves making short-term adjustments to the portfolio based on changing market conditions, economic outlook, or valuation metrics. Tactical asset allocation may involve overweighting or underweighting certain asset classes temporarily to capitalize on short-term opportunities or mitigate risks.

6. **Rebalancing and Monitoring:** Regular monitoring and rebalancing of the investment portfolio are essential components of asset allocation. Rebalancing involves adjusting the portfolio's asset allocation periodically to bring it back in line with the target allocation. Rebalancing helps maintain diversification, control risk exposure, and capitalize on opportunities for growth while minimizing the impact of market volatility.

7. **Tax Considerations:** Asset allocation should also take into account tax implications, such as capital gains taxes, dividend taxes, and tax-deferred

or tax-advantaged investment accounts. Tax-efficient asset location strategies, such as placing tax-inefficient assets in tax-deferred accounts and tax-efficient assets in taxable accounts, can optimize after-tax returns and minimize tax liabilities.

8. **Review and Adjustments:** Asset allocation is not a one-time decision but an ongoing process that requires regular review and adjustments. As an investor's financial situation, goals, and market conditions change, asset allocation may need to be modified accordingly. Periodically reassess your investment objectives, risk tolerance, and market outlook to ensure that your asset allocation remains aligned with your goals and objectives.

In conclusion, asset allocation is a fundamental strategy for achieving a balanced and diversified investment portfolio that aligns with an investor's financial goals and risk tolerance. By determining the right mix of asset classes, maintaining a long-term perspective, diversifying across different investments, regularly monitoring and rebalancing the portfolio, and considering tax implications, investors can optimize risk-adjusted returns and achieve long-term financial success.

- Leveraging the Power of Compound Interest

Leveraging the power of compound interest is a fundamental strategy for building wealth and achieving long-term financial success. Compound interest refers to the process by which the interest earned on an investment or savings account is reinvested, allowing the investment to grow exponentially over time. Here, we'll comprehensively discuss compound interest and how to leverage its power:

1. Understanding Compound Interest:
Compound interest is the concept of earning interest on both the initial principal amount and the accumulated interest from previous periods. As the investment grows, the amount of interest earned also increases, leading to exponential growth over

time. Compound interest allows investments to grow faster than simple interest, where interest is only earned on the principal amount.

2. **The Power of Time:** The key factor in leveraging compound interest is time. The longer the time horizon, the greater the impact of compound interest on investment growth. By starting to invest early and allowing investments to compound over a longer period, investors can benefit from the exponential growth potential of compound interest. Time allows even small contributions to grow into substantial sums over the long term.

3. **Start Early:** One of the most effective ways to leverage compound interest is to start investing as early as possible. Even small contributions made regularly can grow significantly over time due to the power of compounding. By starting early, investors can take advantage of the longest possible time horizon and maximize the growth potential of their investments.

4. **Consistent Contributions:** Consistently contributing to investments or savings accounts is another key strategy for leveraging compound interest. Regular contributions add to the initial principal amount, allowing compound interest to accumulate on a larger base. Automating contributions through payroll deductions or automatic transfers can help ensure consistency and discipline in saving and investing.

5. **Reinvesting Dividends and Interest:** Reinvesting dividends, interest, or other investment income is essential for harnessing the full power of compound interest. Instead of withdrawing investment gains, reinvest them back into the portfolio to compound over time. Reinvesting dividends and interest allows investors to accelerate the growth of their investments and maximize long-term returns.

6. **Compounding Frequencies:** The frequency at which interest is compounded can also impact investment growth. Investments that compound more frequently, such as daily or monthly, will

accumulate interest at a faster rate compared to those that compound less frequently, such as annually. When selecting investment vehicles, consider the compounding frequency and its potential impact on investment growth.

7. **Compound Interest and Risk:** While compound interest can significantly enhance investment returns over the long term, it's essential to consider the role of risk. Higher-risk investments may offer greater growth potential but also come with increased volatility and the potential for loss. Investors should carefully balance risk and return objectives when leveraging compound interest and consider their risk tolerance and investment time horizon.

8. **Patience and Discipline:** Leveraging compound interest requires patience and discipline. It's important to stay focused on long-term goals and resist the temptation to withdraw or reallocate investments based on short-term market fluctuations. Maintaining a disciplined approach to saving and investing, coupled with a long-term

perspective, is key to maximizing the benefits of compound interest.

In conclusion, compound interest is a powerful force that can exponentially grow investments over time. By starting early, making consistent contributions, reinvesting dividends and interest, considering compounding frequencies, balancing risk and return objectives, and maintaining patience and discipline, investors can leverage the power of compound interest to build wealth and achieve their long-term financial goals.

CHAPTER 4:

NAVIGATING THE

INVESTMENT

LANDSCAPE

Welcome to the chapter dedicated to navigating the investment landscape. In today's dynamic and ever-changing financial markets, investors face a myriad of options, opportunities, and challenges when it comes to managing their portfolios and making investment decisions. This chapter is designed to provide you with valuable insights, strategies, and tools to navigate the complexities of the investment landscape with confidence and clarity.

Whether you're a seasoned investor seeking to fine-tune your portfolio or a novice investor looking to get started, this chapter offers comprehensive guidance to help you navigate the intricacies of the investment landscape effectively. From understanding different investment vehicles and asset classes to managing risk, evaluating investment opportunities, and building a diversified portfolio, we'll cover key concepts and principles to empower you to make informed investment decisions.

Navigating the investment landscape requires a combination of knowledge, skill, and judgment. By equipping yourself with the right information and adopting a disciplined approach to investing, you can navigate through market volatility, economic uncertainties, and changing market conditions while striving to achieve your financial goals.

So, join us as we embark on this enlightening journey through the investment landscape. Whether you're seeking to grow your wealth, preserve capital, generate income, or achieve financial independence, this chapter provides valuable insights and strategies to help you navigate the complexities of the investment world and make sound investment decisions that align with your objectives and risk tolerance.

- Stocks: The Cornerstone of Investment Portfolios

Stocks are often considered the cornerstone of investment portfolios due to their potential for long-term capital appreciation and historically higher returns compared to other asset classes. Investing in stocks entails purchasing ownership stakes in publicly traded companies, allowing investors to participate in the company's growth, profitability, and success. Here, we'll comprehensively discuss stocks and their role as the cornerstone of investment portfolios:

1. **Ownership in Companies:** Stocks represent ownership shares in companies, giving investors a claim on the company's assets and earnings. As shareholders, investors have the right to vote on corporate governance matters, such as electing the board of directors and approving major corporate decisions. Owning stocks allows investors to share

in the company's profits through dividends and capital appreciation.

2. **Potential for Growth:** One of the primary reasons stocks are considered the cornerstone of investment portfolios is their potential for long-term growth. Historically, stocks have delivered higher average returns compared to other asset classes, such as bonds or cash equivalents. Investing in well-managed companies with strong growth prospects can lead to significant capital appreciation over time, allowing investors to build wealth and achieve their financial goals.

3. **Diversification Benefits:** Stocks offer diversification benefits by providing exposure to a broad range of industries, sectors, and geographic regions. By investing in a diversified portfolio of stocks, investors can spread their risks across different companies and sectors, reducing the impact of individual company-specific factors on overall portfolio performance. Diversification helps mitigate risk and enhance the stability of investment portfolios.

4. **Liquidity and Market Efficiency:** Stocks are highly liquid assets, meaning they can be bought and sold easily on public stock exchanges. The liquidity of stocks allows investors to quickly convert their investments into cash without significant transaction costs or delays. Moreover, stock markets are highly efficient, incorporating vast amounts of information and reflecting the collective wisdom of millions of investors. As a result, stock prices are continuously adjusted to reflect new information and expectations, ensuring fair and transparent pricing.

5. **Income Generation:** In addition to capital appreciation, stocks can also provide income in the form of dividends. Many companies distribute a portion of their profits to shareholders in the form of cash dividends, providing investors with a steady stream of income. Dividend-paying stocks can be particularly attractive for income-oriented investors seeking regular cash flow and dividend growth over time.

6. **Risks and Volatility:** Despite their potential for growth and income generation, stocks are also subject to various risks and volatility. Stock prices can fluctuate widely in response to changes in market conditions, economic trends, company-specific factors, and geopolitical events. Investors may experience periods of market volatility and downturns, which can result in temporary declines in portfolio value. Understanding and managing risks is essential for successful long-term investing in stocks.

7. **Investment Strategies:** There are different investment strategies for investing in stocks, catering to investors with varying risk tolerances, objectives, and investment horizons. Some investors may adopt a value investing approach, focusing on undervalued companies with strong fundamentals and attractive valuation metrics. Others may prefer growth investing, targeting companies with high growth potential and earnings momentum. Additionally, investors may choose to invest in

specific sectors, industries, or geographic regions based on their investment outlook and preferences.

8. **Long-Term Perspective:** Investing in stocks requires a long-term perspective and patience. While stocks can provide significant returns over time, they also entail short-term volatility and fluctuations. Successful stock investing involves staying disciplined, avoiding emotional reactions to market movements, and maintaining a focus on long-term investment objectives. By adhering to a well-thought-out investment plan and remaining committed to the principles of diversification and risk management, investors can harness the potential of stocks as the cornerstone of their investment portfolios.

In conclusion, stocks play a central role in investment portfolios due to their potential for long-term growth, income generation, diversification benefits, and liquidity. By investing in stocks, investors can participate in the success of leading companies and capitalize on opportunities for wealth creation over time. However, it's essential to understand the risks associated with stock investing and adopt a disciplined approach to portfolio management to achieve long-term financial success.

- Bonds and Fixed-Income Securities

Bonds and fixed-income securities are essential components of investment portfolios, valued for their income generation, capital preservation, and diversification benefits. These securities represent debt obligations issued by governments, corporations, municipalities, or other entities, providing investors with regular interest payments and the return of principal at maturity. Here, we'll comprehensively discuss bonds and fixed-income securities:

1. **Definition and Characteristics:** Bonds are debt instruments that represent loans made by investors to issuers, typically governments or corporations, in exchange for regular interest payments and the return of principal at maturity. Fixed-income

securities refer to a broader category of debt instruments, including bonds, Treasury securities, mortgage-backed securities, corporate bonds, municipal bonds, and other debt obligations. Fixed-income securities are characterized by fixed or predetermined interest payments and a defined maturity date.

2. **Income Generation:** One of the primary attractions of bonds and fixed-income securities is their ability to generate stable and predictable income for investors. Bondholders receive periodic interest payments, usually semiannually or annually, based on the coupon rate specified at the time of issuance. These interest payments provide investors with a reliable source of income, making bonds particularly attractive for income-oriented investors seeking regular cash flow.

3. **Preservation of Capital:** Bonds are often valued for their capital preservation characteristics, offering a lower level of risk compared to stocks and other equity investments. Unlike stocks, which are subject to market fluctuations and volatility,

bonds provide a fixed income stream and return of principal at maturity, making them less volatile and more suitable for capital preservation objectives. Bonds can help investors preserve their capital and mitigate the impact of market downturns or economic uncertainties.

4. **Diversification Benefits:** Fixed-income securities offer diversification benefits by providing exposure to asset classes with low or negative correlations to stocks and other riskier investments. By including bonds in a diversified investment portfolio, investors can spread their risks across different asset classes and reduce portfolio volatility. Diversification helps enhance the stability and resilience of investment portfolios, particularly during periods of market turbulence or economic downturns.

5. **Risk and Return Profile:** While bonds are generally considered less risky than stocks, they are not risk-free investments. Bonds are subject to various risks, including interest rate risk, credit risk, inflation risk, liquidity risk, and call risk. Interest

rate risk refers to the risk of declining bond prices due to changes in interest rates. Credit risk refers to the risk of default by the bond issuer, leading to loss of principal and missed interest payments. Investors should carefully assess the risk-return profile of bonds and fixed-income securities and consider their risk tolerance and investment objectives when incorporating them into their portfolios.

6. **Types of Bonds:** There are several types of bonds and fixed-income securities, each with its unique characteristics, features, and risk profiles:

- **Government Bonds:** Issued by governments to finance public spending and infrastructure projects. Examples include U.S. Treasury bonds, notes, and bills.

- **Corporate Bonds:** Issued by corporations to raise capital for business operations, expansion, or debt refinancing. Corporate bonds offer higher yields than government bonds but carry higher credit risk.

- **Municipal Bonds:** Issued by state and local governments to fund public projects such as schools, roads, and utilities. Municipal bonds offer tax advantages and may be exempt from federal and state income taxes.

- **Agency Bonds:** Issued by government-sponsored enterprises (GSEs) such as Fannie Mae and Freddie Mac to finance housing-related activities. Agency bonds are backed by the issuing agency's credit but may not be explicitly guaranteed by the government.

7. **Yield and Yield Curve:** The yield on a bond represents the annualized return on investment, expressed as a percentage of the bond's face value. Yield is influenced by factors such as prevailing interest rates, bond prices, credit quality, and maturity. The yield curve illustrates the relationship between bond yields and their maturities, providing insights into market expectations for future interest rates and economic conditions.

8. **Duration and Convexity:** Duration and convexity are measures of bond price sensitivity to changes in interest rates. Duration measures the bond's sensitivity to changes in interest rates, with longer-duration bonds exhibiting greater price volatility. Convexity measures the curvature of the bond price-yield relationship and provides additional insights into the bond's price sensitivity. Understanding duration and convexity is essential for managing interest rate risk and optimizing bond portfolio performance.

In conclusion, bonds and fixed-income securities play a crucial role in investment portfolios, offering income generation, capital preservation, and diversification benefits. By including bonds in a diversified investment portfolio, investors can achieve a balanced mix of risk and return and enhance the stability and resilience of their portfolios. However, it's essential to understand the risks associated with bonds and fixed-income securities and carefully evaluate their risk-return profiles to align with investment objectives and preferences.

- Real Estate Investment Strategies

Real estate investment strategies encompass a diverse range of approaches aimed at generating income, capital appreciation, or both through the acquisition, ownership, and management of real estate properties. Real estate investments offer various opportunities for investors to build wealth, diversify portfolios, and achieve long-term financial goals. Here, we'll comprehensively discuss real estate investment strategies:

1. **Rental Properties:** Investing in rental properties involves purchasing residential or commercial real estate properties to rent them out to tenants. Rental properties generate rental income, which can provide a steady stream of cash flow for investors. The rental income from tenants can cover mortgage payments, property taxes, maintenance costs, and

other expenses, allowing investors to build equity and potentially earn a profit over time.

2. **Fix-and-Flip:** Fix-and-flip investing involves purchasing distressed or undervalued properties, renovating or improving them, and selling them for a profit within a relatively short period. Fix-and-flip investors typically look for properties with renovation potential and opportunities to add value through cosmetic upgrades, repairs, or renovations. Successful fix-and-flip investors can capitalize on market inefficiencies, property mispricing, and demand for renovated properties in desirable locations.

3. **Real Estate Investment Trusts (REITs):** REITs are publicly traded companies that own, operate, or finance income-generating real estate properties. REITs provide investors with an opportunity to invest in real estate without directly owning or managing properties. REITs typically specialize in specific property types, such as residential, commercial, retail, or industrial properties. Investing in REITs offers diversification, liquidity,

and potential income through dividends paid to shareholders.

4. **Real Estate Crowdfunding:** Real estate crowdfunding platforms allow investors to pool their capital to invest in real estate projects or properties. Crowdfunding platforms connect investors with real estate developers or operators seeking financing for new developments, acquisitions, or renovations. Real estate crowdfunding offers accessibility, diversification, and potential returns for investors with lower capital requirements compared to traditional real estate investments.

5. **Real Estate Partnerships:** Real estate partnerships involve collaborating with other investors or partners to acquire and manage real estate properties jointly. Real estate partnerships may take various forms, such as limited partnerships, joint ventures, or syndications, depending on the structure and objectives of the investment. Partnering with other investors allows individuals to pool resources, share expertise, and

access larger or more lucrative real estate opportunities.

6. **Vacation Rentals:** Investing in vacation rentals involves purchasing properties in popular tourist destinations and renting them out to vacationers on a short-term basis. Vacation rentals can generate higher rental income compared to traditional long-term rentals, particularly during peak travel seasons. Investors may use online platforms such as Airbnb or VRBO to market their vacation rentals and manage bookings efficiently.

7. **Commercial Real Estate:** Commercial real estate investing involves owning, leasing, or managing commercial properties such as office buildings, retail centers, industrial warehouses, or multifamily apartment complexes. Commercial properties offer the potential for higher rental income, longer lease terms, and lower tenant turnover compared to residential properties. Commercial real estate investors may focus on specific property types or geographic markets based on market dynamics and investment objectives.

8. **Long-Term Buy-and-Hold:** Long-term buy-and-hold investing involves acquiring real estate properties to hold them for an extended period, typically five years or more. Buy-and-hold investors focus on generating rental income, building equity, and benefiting from long-term appreciation in property values. Long-term buy-and-hold investing allows investors to capitalize on the benefits of property ownership, such as tax advantages, inflation hedging, and wealth accumulation over time.

9. **Value-Add Strategies:** Value-add real estate strategies involve identifying properties with potential for value enhancement through strategic renovations, repositioning, or operational improvements. Value-add investors seek properties that are underperforming or have untapped potential, aiming to increase rental income, improve property aesthetics, or enhance tenant amenities to maximize property value and returns.

10. **Geographic and Sectoral Focus:** Real estate investors may choose to focus on specific

geographic regions or sectors based on market dynamics, demographic trends, or investment preferences. Geographic focus may include urban vs. suburban markets, primary vs. secondary markets, or international vs. domestic markets. Sectoral focus may include residential vs. commercial properties, retail vs. industrial properties, or specialized niches such as healthcare, hospitality, or senior housing.

In conclusion, real estate investment strategies offer a wide array of opportunities for investors to generate income, build wealth, and achieve financial goals. Whether through rental properties, fix-and-flip projects, REITs, crowdfunding, partnerships, vacation rentals, commercial properties, or long-term buy-and-hold investments, real estate offers diversification, income, and potential for capital appreciation. Successful real estate investing requires careful research, due diligence, risk management, and alignment with investment objectives and preferences. By understanding the various real estate investment strategies and market dynamics, investors can make informed decisions and build a robust real estate portfolio tailored to their goals and risk tolerance.

- Exploring Alternative Investments

Exploring alternative investments involves diversifying portfolios beyond traditional asset classes such as stocks, bonds, and cash equivalents to include non-traditional or unconventional investment opportunities. Alternative investments offer unique risk-return profiles, potential for capital appreciation, and diversification benefits, complementing traditional investments and providing opportunities for enhanced portfolio performance. Here, we'll comprehensively discuss alternative investments:

1. **Definition and Characteristics:** Alternative investments encompass a wide range of investment opportunities that fall outside the traditional asset classes of stocks, bonds, and cash equivalents.

These investments may include real assets such as real estate, commodities, and infrastructure; hedge funds, private equity, venture capital, and other private investments; as well as structured products, derivatives, collectables, and cryptocurrencies. Alternative investments are characterized by their non-correlation with traditional markets, potential for higher returns, and unique risk factors.

2. **Diversification Benefits:** Alternative investments offer diversification benefits by providing exposure to asset classes with low or negative correlations to traditional stocks and bonds. Including alternative investments in a diversified portfolio can help reduce portfolio volatility, enhance risk-adjusted returns, and mitigate the impact of market downturns or economic uncertainties. By diversifying across different asset classes, investors can spread their risks and achieve a more balanced and resilient portfolio.

3. **Potential for Capital Appreciation:** Alternative investments may offer the potential for capital

appreciation and long-term growth opportunities. Investments such as real estate, private equity, and venture capital can provide access to unique market segments, emerging industries, and high-growth companies that may not be available through traditional investment channels. Alternative investments can generate alpha, or excess returns, through active management, specialized expertise, and market inefficiencies.

4. **Illiquidity and Lock-Up Periods:** One of the key characteristics of alternative investments is their relatively illiquid nature and longer investment horizon compared to traditional investments. Many alternative investments, such as private equity, hedge funds, and real estate partnerships, have lock-up periods or restrictions on redemption, requiring investors to commit their capital for an extended period. Illiquidity risk is an important consideration for investors when allocating capital to alternative investments, as it may impact portfolio liquidity and flexibility.

5. **Risk Factors and Due Diligence:** Alternative investments entail unique risk factors and complexities that require thorough due diligence and risk assessment. Risks associated with alternative investments may include operational risk, regulatory risk, valuation risk, liquidity risk, and manager risk. Investors should conduct comprehensive research, evaluate investment opportunities carefully, and assess the expertise, track record, and integrity of investment managers or sponsors before committing capital to alternative investments.

6. **Access and Investment Structures:** Access to alternative investments may be limited to accredited investors or institutional investors due to regulatory restrictions or minimum investment requirements. Alternative investments are typically accessed through specialized investment vehicles such as private equity funds, hedge funds, real estate investment trusts (REITs), private placements, or crowdfunding platforms. These investment structures may offer varying degrees of

transparency, liquidity, and fee structures, depending on the investment vehicle and strategy.

7. **Performance and Benchmarking:** Evaluating the performance of alternative investments can be challenging due to the lack of standardized benchmarks and transparency compared to traditional asset classes. Alternative investments may be benchmarked against specialized indices, peer groups, or customized benchmarks that reflect the unique characteristics and risk factors of the investment strategy. Investors should carefully monitor the performance of alternative investments, assess their contribution to overall portfolio performance, and adjust allocations based on evolving market conditions and investment objectives.

8. **Regulatory and Tax Considerations:** Alternative investments are subject to regulatory oversight and tax implications that may differ from traditional investments. Regulatory requirements, reporting standards, and tax treatment vary by jurisdiction and investment structure, impacting

investment returns and compliance obligations. Investors should consult with legal, tax, and financial advisors to understand the regulatory and tax considerations associated with alternative investments and optimize their investment strategies accordingly.

9. **Emerging Trends and Innovations:** The landscape of alternative investments is continuously evolving, driven by emerging trends, technological advancements, and market innovations. Alternative investments may include emerging asset classes such as digital assets, blockchain technology, sustainable investing, impact investing, and environmental, social, and governance (ESG) strategies. Investors should stay informed about emerging trends and innovations in alternative investments and evaluate opportunities that align with their investment objectives and values.

In conclusion, exploring alternative investments offers investors opportunities to diversify portfolios, enhance returns, and access unique market segments beyond traditional asset classes. By incorporating alternative investments such as real assets, private investments, structured products, and emerging trends into diversified portfolios, investors can build resilient portfolios, manage risks, and pursue long-term financial goals. However, alternative investments entail complexities, illiquidity, and unique risk factors that require careful due diligence, expertise, and risk management. By understanding the characteristics, opportunities, and challenges of alternative investments, investors can make informed decisions and optimize their investment strategies for long-term success.

CHAPTER 5: THRIVING IN TURBULENT MARKETS

Welcome to the chapter dedicated to thriving in turbulent markets. In today's dynamic and interconnected global economy, financial markets are often characterized by volatility, uncertainty, and rapid changes. Turbulent markets can be triggered by various factors, including geopolitical tensions, economic downturns, technological disruptions, and natural disasters, among others. However, despite the challenges posed by turbulent markets, they also present opportunities for savvy investors to navigate volatility, capitalize on mispricings, and achieve superior investment returns.

In this chapter, we will explore strategies, insights, and techniques to help investors thrive in turbulent markets. Whether you're a seasoned investor seeking to adapt to changing market conditions or a novice investor looking to understand how to navigate volatility, this chapter provides valuable guidance to help you succeed in turbulent times.

We'll discuss various topics, including risk management strategies, asset allocation techniques, behavioral finance principles, and tactical approaches to capitalize on market opportunities. By understanding the dynamics of turbulent markets and adopting a proactive and disciplined approach to investing, investors can position themselves to not only survive but thrive in volatile environments.

So, join us as we delve into the strategies and insights that can empower you to navigate turbulent markets successfully, seize opportunities, and achieve your financial goals amidst uncertainty and volatility. Whether you're facing market downturns, economic crises, or unexpected disruptions, this chapter equips you with the knowledge and tools to thrive and prosper in turbulent times.

- Understanding Market Cycles

Understanding market cycles is essential for investors to navigate the ups and downs of financial markets effectively. Market cycles refer to the recurring patterns of expansion and contraction in asset prices and economic activity over time. By recognizing and understanding the different phases of market cycles, investors can make informed decisions, manage risk, and capitalize on opportunities. Here, we'll comprehensively discuss market cycles:

1. **Phases of Market Cycles:**

   - **Expansion**: The expansion phase, also known as the bull market, is characterized by rising asset prices, strong economic growth, increasing corporate profits, and optimistic investor sentiment. During this phase, demand for investments is high, and risk appetite is elevated. Bull markets are typically fueled by factors such as low-interest rates, favorable economic conditions, and positive market sentiment.

- **Peak:** The peak marks the culmination of the expansion phase, where asset prices reach their highest levels and investor optimism peaks. At the peak, valuations may become stretched, and speculative excesses may emerge. Market participants may become overconfident, leading to euphoria and irrational exuberance. Peaks are often followed by periods of consolidation or correction as market sentiment shifts.

- **Contraction:** The contraction phase, also known as the bear market, is characterized by declining asset prices, economic slowdown or recession, falling corporate profits, and pessimistic investor sentiment. During this phase, fear and uncertainty dominate the market, leading to risk aversion and selling pressure. Bear markets are typically accompanied by factors such as rising interest rates, deteriorating economic indicators, and negative news flow.

- **Trough:** The trough marks the bottom of the contraction phase, where asset prices reach their lowest levels, and investor pessimism reaches a nadir. At the trough, valuations may become depressed, and sentiment may be extremely negative. However, troughs also present opportunities for savvy investors to identify undervalued assets and position themselves for potential recovery.

2. **Drivers of Market Cycles:**

- **Economic Indicators:** Market cycles are closely tied to economic cycles, as changes in economic indicators such as GDP growth, unemployment rates, inflation, and consumer spending influence investor sentiment and market dynamics.

- **Monetary Policy:** Central bank policies, including interest rate decisions, monetary stimulus measures, and quantitative easing programs, can impact market cycles by influencing borrowing costs, liquidity conditions, and investor behavior.

- Corporate Earnings: Corporate earnings growth is a key driver of market cycles, as improving or deteriorating earnings prospects can impact investor expectations and asset valuations.

- Geopolitical Events: Geopolitical tensions, trade disputes, geopolitical conflicts, and other global events can disrupt market cycles by introducing uncertainty, volatility, and risk aversion among investors.

- Psychological Factors: Investor sentiment, emotions, and behavioral biases play a significant role in driving market cycles, as fear, greed, optimism, and pessimism can influence market trends and price movements.

3. **Characteristics of Different Asset Classes:**

- Stocks: Equity markets are highly cyclical, experiencing periods of bull markets and bear markets driven by economic and corporate fundamentals, investor sentiment, and market dynamics.

- **Bonds:** Fixed-income markets exhibit cyclical patterns influenced by changes in interest rates, inflation expectations, credit conditions, and central bank policies.

- **Commodities:** Commodity markets are cyclical due to supply and demand dynamics, geopolitical factors, weather patterns, and currency fluctuations affecting commodity prices.

- **Real Estate:** Real estate markets go through cycles of expansion and contraction influenced by factors such as interest rates, housing demand, population growth, and construction activity.

4. **Strategies for Navigating Market Cycles:**

- **Asset Allocation:** Diversification across asset classes can help investors manage risk and mitigate the impact of market cycles on portfolio performance.

- **Tactical Asset Allocation:** Adjusting portfolio allocations based on market conditions, economic indicators, and valuations can help investors capitalize on opportunities and mitigate risks during different phases of market cycles.

- **Risk Management:** Implementing risk management strategies such as stop-loss orders, position sizing, and portfolio rebalancing can help investors protect capital and limit downside risk during market downturns.

- **Long-Term Perspective:** Maintaining a long-term investment horizon and avoiding emotional reactions to short-term market fluctuations can help investors stay disciplined and focused on their investment objectives throughout market cycles.

- **Contrarian Investing:** Contrarian investors seek to capitalize on market cycles by buying undervalued assets during bear markets and selling overvalued assets during bull markets. Contrarian strategies involve going against the crowd and taking advantage of market inefficiencies and mispricings.

In conclusion, understanding market cycles is essential for investors to navigate the complexities of financial markets effectively. By recognizing the different phases of market cycles, understanding the drivers of market movements, and implementing appropriate investment strategies, investors can manage risk, capitalize on opportunities, and achieve long-term financial success amidst changing market conditions. While market cycles are inevitable and unpredictable, a disciplined and informed approach to investing can help investors thrive across various market environments.

- Strategies for Managing Market Volatility

Managing market volatility is crucial for investors to navigate turbulent market conditions effectively and protect their portfolios from excessive fluctuations. Market volatility refers to the degree of variation in asset prices over time, often characterized by rapid and unpredictable price swings. Here, we'll comprehensively discuss strategies for managing market volatility:

1. Diversification:

- Diversification involves spreading investments across different asset classes, sectors, industries, and geographic regions to reduce the impact of volatility on portfolio performance.

- By diversifying investments, investors can mitigate the risk of significant losses from adverse movements in any single asset or market segment.

- Diversification helps smooth out portfolio returns and enhances the stability and resilience of investment portfolios across various market conditions.

2. Asset Allocation:

- Asset allocation involves determining the optimal mix of asset classes (e.g., stocks, bonds, cash equivalents, real estate) based on investment objectives, risk tolerance, and time horizon.

- Adopting a strategic asset allocation approach that aligns with long-term financial goals can help investors manage market volatility and achieve a balanced risk-return profile.

- Asset allocation strategies may involve adjusting portfolio weights based on changing market conditions, economic outlook, and valuation metrics to optimize risk-adjusted returns.

3. Active Risk Management:

- Implementing active risk management strategies can help investors mitigate the impact of market volatility on portfolio performance.

- Setting stop-loss orders, implementing trailing stop orders, or using options strategies such as protective puts can help limit downside risk and protect capital during market downturns.

- Regular portfolio monitoring, rebalancing, and adjusting exposure to different asset classes based on risk assessments and market conditions can help investors adapt to changing volatility levels.

4. Focus on Fundamentals:

- Maintaining a focus on fundamental analysis and underlying investment fundamentals can help investors navigate market volatility with confidence.

- Investing in fundamentally sound companies with strong financials, competitive advantages, and sustainable business models can provide resilience against short-term market fluctuations.

- Fundamental analysis involves assessing factors such as revenue growth, earnings stability, cash flow generation, balance sheet strength, and management quality to identify high-quality investment opportunities.

5. Long-Term Perspective:

- Adopting a long-term investment horizon and resisting the temptation to react impulsively to short-term market volatility can help investors stay focused on their long-term financial goals.

- Markets may experience periods of heightened volatility and uncertainty, but maintaining a disciplined approach to investing and staying committed to long-term objectives can help investors ride out market fluctuations.

- Historically, long-term investors who remain patient and disciplined during volatile market environments have been rewarded with positive investment returns over time.

6. Dollar-Cost Averaging:

- Dollar-cost averaging involves investing a fixed amount of money at regular intervals, regardless of market conditions.

- By dollar-cost averaging, investors can take advantage of market volatility by purchasing more shares when prices are low and fewer shares when prices are high, effectively averaging out the cost per share over time.

- Dollar-cost averaging can help mitigate the impact of market timing decisions and reduce the risk of making large, concentrated investments at unfavorable price levels.

7. Stress Testing and Scenario Analysis:

- Conducting stress testing and scenario analysis can help investors assess the potential impact of extreme market events and develop contingency plans to manage volatility.

- By simulating different market scenarios and stress-testing portfolio holdings under adverse conditions, investors can identify vulnerabilities, assess risk exposures, and implement proactive risk management measures.

- Scenario analysis enables investors to anticipate potential outcomes, adjust portfolio allocations accordingly, and position themselves to withstand market shocks effectively.

8. Seek Professional Advice:

- Seeking professional advice from financial advisors, wealth managers, or investment professionals can provide valuable insights, guidance, and expertise in managing market volatility.

- Financial professionals can help investors develop customized investment strategies, construct diversified portfolios, and implement risk management techniques tailored to individual needs and preferences.

- Collaborating with trusted advisors can provide investors with peace of mind, confidence, and support in navigating turbulent market conditions and achieving their financial objectives.

In conclusion, managing market volatility requires a combination of prudent investment strategies, risk management techniques, and disciplined execution. By diversifying portfolios, optimizing asset allocation, implementing active risk management, focusing on fundamentals, maintaining a long-term perspective, utilizing dollar-cost averaging, conducting stress testing, and seeking professional advice, investors can effectively navigate turbulent market environments and position themselves for long-term financial success. While market volatility is inevitable, investors who adopt a proactive and disciplined approach to managing volatility can mitigate risks, seize opportunities, and achieve their investment goals over time.

- Importance of Rebalancing Your Portfolio

Rebalancing your portfolio is a critical component of prudent portfolio management and essential for maintaining an optimal risk-return profile over time. Rebalancing involves periodically adjusting the asset allocation of your investment portfolio back to your target allocation to ensure alignment with your investment objectives, risk tolerance, and long-term financial goals. Here, we'll comprehensively discuss the importance of rebalancing your portfolio:

1. Maintaining Asset Allocation Targets:

- Rebalancing helps investors maintain their desired asset allocation targets by periodically realigning the portfolio's composition with the original target weights for different asset classes (e.g., stocks, bonds, cash equivalents).

- Over time, changes in asset prices and market performance can cause the portfolio's asset allocation to deviate from the target allocation. Rebalancing ensures that the portfolio remains consistent with the investor's risk tolerance and investment strategy.

2. Risk Management:

- Rebalancing helps manage portfolio risk by reducing exposure to asset classes that have become overweight due to strong performance and increasing exposure to asset classes that have become underweight due to weaker performance.

- By rebalancing, investors can mitigate the risk of portfolio concentration in over performing assets and avoid unintended exposure to excessive risk factors, ensuring diversification and risk control.

3. Minimizing Drift:

- Portfolio drift occurs when the actual asset allocation deviates significantly from the target allocation over time. Drift can occur due to market fluctuations, changes in asset prices, cash flows, or portfolio rebalancing.

- Rebalancing helps minimize drift by periodically adjusting the portfolio's asset allocation to bring it back in line with the target allocation, preventing unintended shifts in risk exposure and portfolio characteristics.

4. Capturing Rebalancing Premium:

- Research has shown that rebalancing portfolios can lead to improved risk-adjusted returns over time, a phenomenon known as the rebalancing premium.

- Rebalancing involves selling assets that have appreciated and buying assets that have declined in value, effectively buying low and selling high. This contrarian approach can enhance portfolio returns by capitalizing on mean reversion and market inefficiencies.

5. **Enhancing Long-Term Performance:**

- Rebalancing contributes to the long-term performance of the portfolio by ensuring that investment decisions are based on a disciplined and systematic approach rather than emotional reactions to short-term market fluctuations.

- While rebalancing may result in short-term transaction costs and tax implications, it can lead to improved risk-adjusted returns and smoother portfolio performance over the long term.

6. **Adapting to Changing Market Conditions:**

- Rebalancing allows investors to adapt to changing market conditions, economic outlooks, and investment trends by periodically reassessing their asset allocation and adjusting portfolio weights accordingly.

- Market environments are dynamic, and asset classes may perform differently over time. Rebalancing ensures that the portfolio remains responsive to evolving market dynamics and macroeconomic factors.

7. **Aligning with Investment Goals:**

- Rebalancing ensures that the portfolio remains aligned with the investor's investment goals, time horizon, and risk tolerance. As investors' financial circumstances, objectives, and risk preferences evolve, periodic rebalancing helps realign the portfolio with changing needs and priorities.

- Whether the goal is capital preservation, income generation, wealth accumulation, or retirement planning, rebalancing ensures that the portfolio remains on track to achieve long-term financial objectives.

8. **Discipline and Accountability:**

- Rebalancing instills discipline and accountability in the investment process, fostering a systematic and structured approach to portfolio management.

- By establishing a regular rebalancing schedule and adhering to predefined rules and criteria, investors can maintain a disciplined investment strategy and avoid succumbing to emotional biases or market timing errors.

In conclusion, rebalancing your portfolio is a fundamental practice in effective portfolio management, essential for maintaining asset allocation targets, managing risk, minimizing drift, capturing rebalancing premium, enhancing long-term performance, adapting to changing market conditions, aligning with investment goals, and fostering discipline and accountability. While rebalancing may involve transaction costs and tax implications, the benefits of maintaining a well-balanced and diversified portfolio outweigh the associated costs, contributing to long-term investment success and wealth accumulation. Investors should establish a disciplined rebalancing strategy and incorporate rebalancing into their overall investment plan to achieve optimal portfolio outcomes and financial goals over time.

- Investing in Uncertain Times: Opportunities Amidst Challenges

Investing in uncertain times presents both challenges and opportunities for investors. Uncertain economic conditions, geopolitical tensions, market volatility, and global events can create uncertainty and apprehension among investors. However, amidst the challenges, there are also opportunities for savvy investors to capitalize on market inefficiencies, identify undervalued assets, and position themselves for long-term success. Here, we'll comprehensively discuss investing in uncertain times:

1. Volatility as an Opportunity:

- Market volatility is a common characteristic of uncertain times, with asset prices fluctuating more widely than usual. While volatility can be unsettling for investors, it also presents opportunities to buy assets at discounted prices and capitalize on short-term mispricings.

- Volatility-driven market sell-offs may create buying opportunities for investors with a long-term investment horizon, enabling them to acquire quality assets at lower valuations and potentially benefit from future price appreciation.

2. Diversification and Risk Management:

- Diversification is essential for managing risk and mitigating the impact of uncertainty on investment portfolios. By diversifying across different asset classes, sectors, and geographic regions, investors can spread their risks and reduce vulnerability to adverse market events.

- Maintaining a balanced portfolio with a mix of equities, fixed income, cash equivalents, and alternative investments can help investors navigate uncertain times and preserve capital while seeking growth opportunities.

3. Quality Over Quantity:

- In uncertain times, quality investments become particularly important as investors prioritize stability, resilience, and sustainability. Focus on companies with strong fundamentals, robust balance sheets, competitive advantages, and reliable cash flows.

- Quality investments may exhibit greater resilience to economic downturns, market volatility, and geopolitical risks, providing downside protection and potential for long-term outperformance.

4. Long-Term Investment Horizon:

- Maintaining a long-term investment horizon is crucial in uncertain times, as short-term market fluctuations and geopolitical events may cause temporary volatility and noise in financial markets.

- Investors with a long-term perspective can capitalize on market downturns to accumulate quality assets at attractive prices and benefit from compounding returns over time, despite short-term fluctuations.

5. Adaptability and Flexibility:

- Flexibility and adaptability are essential qualities for investors navigating uncertain times. Be prepared to adjust investment strategies, reassess risk tolerances, and reallocate portfolio assets based on changing market conditions and economic outlooks.

- Stay informed about macroeconomic trends, geopolitical developments, and market dynamics, and be willing to make timely adjustments to investment portfolios as warranted by changing circumstances.

6. Contrarian Investing:

- Contrarian investing involves going against the crowd and buying assets that are undervalued or out of favor with the market consensus. In uncertain times, contrarian investors may find opportunities to capitalize on market pessimism and investor sentiment extremes.

- Contrarian strategies require patience, discipline, and conviction to withstand short-term market noise and volatility while waiting for market sentiment to normalize and asset prices to reflect underlying fundamentals.

7. Selective Sector and Geographic Exposure:

- Selective sector and geographic exposure can help investors navigate uncertain times by focusing on industries, regions, or asset classes with favorable growth prospects, resilience to economic shocks, or unique investment opportunities.

- Evaluate sectors and geographic regions based on factors such as demographic trends, technological advancements, regulatory environments, and competitive landscapes to identify areas of potential outperformance in uncertain times.

8. Opportunistic Allocation:

- Opportunistic allocation involves capitalizing on short-term market dislocations, inefficiencies, or market overreactions to identify attractive investment opportunities. In uncertain times, market disruptions may create opportunities for value-oriented investors to deploy capital at favorable terms.

- Maintain liquidity and flexibility in investment portfolios to capitalize on opportunistic allocations and take advantage of market opportunities as they arise.

9. **Risk Assessment and Scenario Analysis:**

- Conducting risk assessment and scenario analysis can help investors anticipate potential outcomes and develop contingency plans to manage risk in uncertain times. Evaluate the potential impact of different economic scenarios, geopolitical events, and market shocks on investment portfolios.

- Scenario analysis enables investors to identify vulnerabilities, assess risk exposures, and implement proactive risk management measures to protect capital and preserve wealth in uncertain environments.

10. **Continuous Learning and Adaptation:**

- Continuous learning and adaptation are essential for investors to navigate uncertain times successfully. Stay informed about market developments, economic trends, and regulatory changes, and be willing to adjust investment strategies based on new information and evolving market conditions.

- Seek advice from financial professionals, participate in educational opportunities, and leverage research resources to enhance investment knowledge and decision-making capabilities in uncertain times.

In conclusion, investing in uncertain times requires a combination of discipline, resilience, and opportunism. While uncertain economic conditions, geopolitical tensions, and market volatility may present challenges for investors, they also create opportunities for those willing to adopt a long-term perspective, prioritize quality investments, remain flexible and adaptable, and capitalize on market inefficiencies. By focusing on diversification, risk management, quality investments, long-term horizons, contrarian strategies, opportunistic allocations, risk assessment, and continuous learning, investors can navigate uncertain times successfully and achieve their financial goals amidst uncertainty and volatility.

CONCLUSION

In conclusion, "Wealth Whispers: Insights into Successful Investing and Financial Growth" has explored the multifaceted world of investing, offering valuable insights, strategies, and principles to guide readers on their journey towards financial prosperity. Throughout this book, we have delved into the fundamental concepts of investing, from understanding market dynamics and managing risk to identifying opportunities and embracing uncertainty.

As investors, we are constantly navigating a dynamic and ever-changing landscape, where markets fluctuate, economies evolve, and geopolitical events unfold. In the face of such uncertainty, the principles outlined in this book serve as a compass, guiding us towards informed decision-making, disciplined execution, and long-term success.

We have emphasized the importance of adopting a holistic approach to investing, one that encompasses asset allocation, diversification, risk management, and disciplined execution. By maintaining a diversified portfolio, staying focused on long-term objectives, and adhering to sound investment principles, readers can mitigate risk, capitalize on opportunities, and achieve their financial goals over time.

Furthermore, we have highlighted the significance of mindset, discipline, and continuous learning in the pursuit of financial growth. Cultivating an abundance mindset, overcoming psychological biases, and embracing risk as an opportunity are essential components of a successful investor's toolkit. Additionally, we have explored the importance of adaptability, flexibility, and resilience in navigating turbulent markets and uncertain times.

Ultimately, "Wealth Whispers" is more than just a book about investing; it is a roadmap for building wealth, achieving financial independence, and realizing one's dreams. Whether you are a novice investor taking your first steps into the world of finance or a seasoned veteran seeking to refine your investment strategy, the insights shared within these pages offer timeless wisdom and actionable advice to help you unlock the secrets to successful investing and financial growth.

As you embark on your investment journey, remember that wealth whispers its secrets to those who listen attentively, who approach investing with humility and respect, and who are committed to the pursuit of excellence. May the insights contained within this book serve as a guiding light on your path to prosperity, empowering you to build a brighter and more secure financial future for yourself and your loved ones.

www.ingramcontent.com/pod-product-compliance
Lightning Source LLC
Chambersburg PA
CBHW060405290526
45791CB00002B/611